DINOSAUR FACT DIG

ALLOSAURUS
AND ITS RELATIVES
THE NEED-TO-KNOW FACTS

BY
MEGAN
COOLEY PETERSON

Consultant: Mathew J. Wedel, PhD
Associate Professor
Western University of Health Services

CAPSTONE PRESS
a capstone imprint

A+ Books are published by Capstone Press,
1710 Roe Crest Drive, North Mankato, Minnesota 56003
www.mycapstone.com

Library of Congress Cataloging-in-Publication Data
Names: Peterson, Megan Cooley, author.
Title: Allosaurus and its relatives: the need-to-know facts / by Megan Cooley Peterson
Description: North Mankato, Minnesota: Capstone Press, [2017] | Series: A+ books.
Dinosaur fact dig | Audience: Ages 6-8. | Audience: K to grade 3. | Includes bibliographical
references and index.
Identifiers: LCCN 2015046629| ISBN 9781515726975 (library binding) | ISBN
9781515727019 (pbk.) | ISBN 9781515727057 (ebook (pdf))
Subjects: LCSH: Saurischia–Juvenile literature. | Dinosaurs–Juvenile literature.
Classification: LCC QE862.S3 C53 2017 | DDC 567.912–dc23
LC record available at http://lccn.loc.gov/2015046629

EDITORIAL CREDITS:

Michelle Hasselius, editor; Kazuko Collins, designer; Wanda Winch, media researcher;
Gene Bentdahl, production specialist

IMAGE CREDITS:

All images by Jon Hughes except: MapArt (maps), Shutterstock: Elena Elisseeva, green
gingko leaf, Jiang Hongyan, yellow gingko leaf, Taigi, paper background

Printed in China.
022016   007586

**NOTE TO PARENTS, TEACHERS,
AND LIBRARIANS:**
This Dinosaur Fact Dig book uses
full-color images and a nonfiction format
to introduce the concept of dinosaurs
related to Allosaurus. *Allosaurus and Its
Relatives* is designed to be read aloud to
a pre-reader or to be read independently
by an early reader. Images help listeners
and early readers understand the text and
concepts discussed. The book encourages
further learning by including the following
sections: Table of Contents, Glossary, Critical
Thinking Using the Common Core, Read
More, Internet Sites, and Index. Early readers
may need assistance using these features.

TABLE OF CONTENTS

Allosaurus was a fearsome, meat-eating dinosaur. Using sawlike teeth and sharp claws, it attacked other dinosaurs. Chomp!

Some of the biggest meat-eating dinosaurs belonged to the Allosaurus family. Carcharodontosaurus and Giganotosaurus may have been even bigger than Tyrannosaurus rex! Read on to learn more about Allosaurus and its relatives.

ACROCANTHOSAURUS

PRONOUNCED: ACK-roh-KAN-thuh-SAWR-us

NAME MEANING: high-spined lizard

TIME PERIOD LIVED: Early Cretaceous Period

LENGTH: 35 feet (11 meters)

WEIGHT: 4.9 tons (4.4 metric tons)

TYPE OF EATER: carnivore

PHYSICAL FEATURES: sail down its back; sharp claws and teeth; strong legs

ACROCANTHOSAURUS was as long as Tyrannosaurus rex but weighed less.

Only four **ACROCANTHOSAURUS** skeletons have been found so far.

Acrocanthosaurus lived in the forests and swamps of what are now Oklahoma, Texas, and Utah.

where this dinosaur lived

ACROCANTHOSAURUS' eyes faced to the side. It cocked its head to one side to see prey.

ALLOSAURUS

PRONOUNCED: AL-uh-SAWR-us

NAME MEANING: strange reptile

TIME PERIOD LIVED: Late Jurassic Period

LENGTH: 28 feet (8.5 m)

WEIGHT: 3 tons (2.7 metric tons)

TYPE OF EATER: carnivore

PHYSICAL FEATURES: long tail; curved claws; traveled on two legs; jagged teeth

ALLOSAURUS was the most common dinosaur in North America during the Late Jurassic Period.

ALLOSAURUS may have hunted in packs. A pack could kill very large prey.

Allosaurus lived on plains in what is now North America.

N
W E
S

where this dinosaur lived

At the Cleveland-Lloyd Quarry in Utah, scientists have found baby **ALLOSAURUS** fossils that are the size of dogs.

AUCASAURUS

PRONOUNCED: AW-ka-SAWR-us

NAME MEANING: Auca lizard; named after Auca Mahuevo, the site where it was discovered

TIME PERIOD LIVED: Late Cretaceous Period

LENGTH: 18 feet (5.5 m)

WEIGHT: 1,500 pounds (680 kilograms)

TYPE OF EATER: carnivore

PHYSICAL FEATURES: sawlike teeth; strong back legs and tail

AUCASAURUS was a fast runner. It could chase prey at high speeds.

AUCASAURUS is one of the best-known meat-eaters. All of its bones have been found except for the ones at the end of its tail.

Aucasaurus lived on the plains of what is now Argentina.

N
W E
S

where this dinosaur lived

AUCASAURUS had very short arms. Its hands were not able to reach each other.

BARYONYX

PRONOUNCED: BEAR-ee-ON-icks

NAME MEANING: heavy claw

TIME PERIOD LIVED: Early Cretaceous Period

LENGTH: 32.8 feet (10 m)

WEIGHT: 1.3 tons (1.2 metric tons)

TYPE OF EATER: carnivore

PHYSICAL FEATURES: long crocodile-like jaw and teeth; big claw on each hand

In 1983 fossil hunter William Walker found the first **BARYONYX** bone. He unearthed a 10-inch- (25-centimeter-) long claw.

Baryonyx lived near the waters of what are now England and Spain.

Partially digested fish bones, scales, and the bones of a baby Iguanodon were found inside a **BARYONYX**.

N
W E
S

where this dinosaur lived

Scientists nicknamed the first **BARYONYX** specimen "Claws."

CARCHARODONTOSAURUS

PRONOUNCED: car-CARE-oh-DON-tuh-SAWR-us

NAME MEANING: shark-tooth lizard

TIME PERIOD LIVED: Late Cretaceous Period

LENGTH: 40 feet (12 m)

WEIGHT: 6.6 tons (6 metric tons)

TYPE OF EATER: carnivore

PHYSICAL FEATURES: large jaw to swallow its prey whole; sharp teeth

CARCHARODONTOSAURUS had a larger skull than Tyrannosaurus rex, but its brain was smaller.

Carcharodontosaurus lived in the deserts and swamps of what are now Algeria, Egypt, Morocco, and Niger.

N
W → E
S

where this dinosaur lived

CARCHARODONTOSAURUS had knifelike teeth about 8 inches (20 cm) long.

A **CARCHARODONTOSAURUS** skull is about 5 feet (1.5 m) long. That's about the size of an

CRYOLOPHOSAURUS

PRONOUNCED: CRY-o-LO-fo-SAWR-us

NAME MEANING: frozen-crested lizard

TIME PERIOD LIVED: Early Jurassic Period

LENGTH: 20 feet (6 m)

WEIGHT: 800 pounds (363 kg)

TYPE OF EATER: carnivore

PHYSICAL FEATURES: sharp teeth; crest on top of its head

A **CRYOLOPHOSAURUS** skeleton was found with rib bones near its throat. At first scientists thought the dinosaur died choking on another animal's bones. Later scientists learned the ribs belonged to the Cryolophosaurus.

CRYOLOPHOSAURUS was one of the biggest meat-eating dinosaurs on Earth during the Early Jurassic Period.

CRYOLOPHOSAURUS' crest resembled a hairstyle worn by the famous singer, Elvis Presley. Some scientists have nicknamed the dinosaur "Elvisaurus."

Cryolophosaurus lived in the forests of what is now Antarctica.

N
W — E
S

where this dinosaur lived

GASOSAURUS

PRONOUNCED: GAS-o-SAWR-us

NAME MEANING: gas lizard

TIME PERIOD LIVED: Middle Jurassic Period

LENGTH: 12 feet (3.7 m)

WEIGHT: 150 pounds (68 kg)

TYPE OF EATER: carnivore

PHYSICAL FEATURES: sharp teeth; big claws; strong back legs

GASOSAURUS used its arms to hold its prey while eating.

In 1972 a company drilling for gas found the only known **GASOSAURUS** fossils. This is how the dinosaur got its name.

Gasosaurus lived in the forests of what is now China.

N
W · E
S

■ where this dinosaur lived

Some scientists believe the partial **GASOSAURUS** skeleton found may have belonged to a young Gasosaurus. The dinosaur's skull has not been found.

GIGANOTOSAURUS

PRONOUNCED: gig-an-O-toe-SAWR-us

NAME MEANING: giant southern reptile

TIME PERIOD LIVED: Late Cretaceous Period

LENGTH: 45 feet (14 m)

WEIGHT: 8.8 tons (8 metric tons)

TYPE OF EATER: carnivore

PHYSICAL FEATURES: sharp teeth and claws; strong legs

GIGANOTOSAURUS' brain was about the size of a banana.

Giganotosaurus lived in the plains and forests of what is now Argentina.

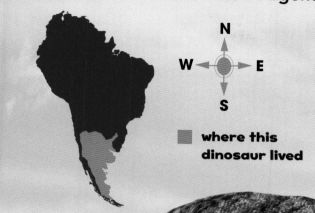

N
W   E
S

■ where this dinosaur lived

GIGANOTOSAURUS' teeth were 8 inches (20 cm) long and serrated like a knife.

Scientists think **GIGANOTOSAURUS** may have been able to run up to 31 miles (50 kilometers) per hour. That's faster than Tyrannosaurus rex.

NEOVENATOR

PRONOUNCED: KNEE-o-vuh-NAY-tur

NAME MEANING: new hunter

TIME PERIOD LIVED: Early Cretaceous Period

LENGTH: 23 feet (7 m)

WEIGHT: 1.1 tons (1 metric ton)

TYPE OF EATER: carnivore

PHYSICAL FEATURES: small crests on its snout; strong neck; sharp claws and teeth

About 70 percent of a complete **NEOVENATOR** skeleton has been found.

Neovenator lived in the swamps of what is now England.

where this dinosaur lived

NEOVENATOR had three clawed toes on each foot.

The first **NEOVENATOR** bones were found in 1978. They were seen sticking out of a cliff on the Isle of Wight in England.

OZRAPTOR

PRONOUNCED: oz-RAP-tur

NAME MEANING: thief of Oz; Oz is short for Ozzies, a nickname for Australians

TIME PERIOD LIVED: Middle Jurassic Period

LENGTH: 6.6 feet (2 m)

WEIGHT: 100 pounds (45 kg)

TYPE OF EATER: carnivore

PHYSICAL FEATURES: powerful jaws; sharp teeth; strong legs; stiff tail used for balance while running

In the mid-1960s, four boys found the first **OZRAPTOR** bone near Geraldton, Australia.

Ozraptor lived in the forests and plains of what is now Australia.

N
W • E
S

where this dinosaur lived

OZRAPTOR was a hunter, but it was also a scavenger. It would eat dead animals.

OZRAPTOR is one of the oldest Australian dinosaurs.

SPINOSAURUS

PRONOUNCED: SPY-nuh-SAWR-us

NAME MEANING: spine reptile

TIME PERIOD LIVED: middle Cretaceous Period

LENGTH: 52.5 feet (16 m)

WEIGHT: 11 tons (10 metric tons)

TYPE OF EATER: carnivore

PHYSICAL FEATURES: sail down its back; long jaw; cone-shaped teeth; paddlelike feet for swimming

SPINOSAURUS spent most of its time in or near water. It splashed into the water looking for prey.

Spinosaurus lived near water in what are now Egypt and Morocco.

N
W · E
S

■ where this dinosaur lived

SPINOSAURUS had nostrils halfway up its snout. This helped it breathe while hunting in the water.

The original SPINOSAURUS specimen that was found in 1912 was destroyed during World War II (1939–1945).

SUCHOMIMUS

PRONOUNCED: SOO-cho-MYE-mus

NAME MEANING: crocodile mimic

TIME PERIOD LIVED: Late Cretaceous Period

LENGTH: 36 feet (11 m)

WEIGHT: 4.9 tons (4.4 metric tons)

TYPE OF EATER: carnivore

PHYSICAL FEATURES: sail; long snout; sharp claws; strong arms

SUCHOMIMUS had nostrils that sat far up on its snout. This may have helped the dinosaur breathe while hunting in the water.

Suchomimus lived near lakes and rivers in what is now Niger, Africa.

N
W · E
S

where this dinosaur lived

SUCHOMIMUS had a 1-foot-(0.3-m-) long thumb claw on each hand.

SUCHOMIMUS' teeth pointed backward to grip slippery fish.

XUANHANOSAURUS

PRONOUNCED: shawn-HAN-o-SAWR-us

NAME MEANING: Xuanhan County reptile; named after the site where it was found

TIME PERIOD LIVED: Middle Jurassic Period

LENGTH: 19.7 feet (6 m)

WEIGHT: 500 pounds (227 kg)

TYPE OF EATER: carnivore

PHYSICAL FEATURES: sharp claws and teeth; strong arms and legs

XUANHANOSAURUS was discovered with a large number of other dinosaur fossils, including Gasosaurus.

Xuanhanosaurus lived in the forests of what is now China.

N
W E
S

where this dinosaur lived

XUANHANOSAURUS is only known from a few bones, including a forelimb and shoulder bone.

XUANHANOSAURUS had three fingers on each hand.

GLOSSARY

CARNIVORE (KAR-nuh-vor)—an animal that eats only meat

CREST (KREST)—a flat plate of bone

CRETACEOUS PERIOD (krah-TAY-shus PIHR-ee-uhd)—the third period of the Mesozoic Era; the Cretaceous Period was from 145 to 65 million years ago

FOSSIL (FOSS-uhl)—the remains of an animal or plant from millions of years ago that have turned to rock

JURASSIC PERIOD (ju-RASS-ik PIHR-ee-uhd)—the second period of the Mesozoic Era; the Jurassic Period was from 200 to 145 million years ago

NOSTRIL (NOSS-truhl)—one of two openings in the nose used to breathe and smell

PLAIN (PLANE)—a large, flat area of land with few trees

PREY (PRAY)—an animal hunted by another animal for food

PRONOUNCE (proh-NOUNSS)—to say a word in a certain way

QUARRY (KWOR-ee)—a place where stone and other materials are dug from the ground

RELATIVE (REL-uh-tive)—a member of a family

SERRATED (SER-ay-tid)—saw-toothed

SNOUT (SNOUT)—the long front part of an animal's head; the snout includes the nose, mouth, and jaws

SPECIMEN (SPESS-uh-muhn)—a sample or an example used to stand for an entire group

WORLD WAR II—a war in which the United States, France, Great Britain, the Soviet Union, and other countries defeated Germany, Italy, and Japan; World War II lasted from 1939 to 1945

CRITICAL THINKING USING THE COMMON CORE

1. Scientists have found Allosaurus fossils at the Cleveland-Lloyd Quarry in Utah. What is a quarry? (Craft and Structure)

2. How did Gasosaurus get its name? Use the text to help you with your answer. (Key Ideas and Details)

3. Suchomimus had nostrils far up on its snout. How did this help the dinosaur hunt for food? (Key Ideas and Details)

READ MORE

Lee, Sally. *Allosaurus.* Little Paleontologist. North Mankato, Minn.: Capstone Press, 2015.

Miller, Henley. *Meet Giganotosaurus.* The Age of Dinosaurs. New York: Cavendish Square, 2015.

Silverman, Buffy. *Can You Tell a Tyrannosaurus from an Allosaurus?* Dinosaur Look-Alikes. Minneapolis: Lerner Publications Company, 2014.

INTERNET SITES

FactHound offers a safe, fun way to find Internet sites related to this book. All of the sites on FactHound have been researched by our staff.

Here's all you do:

Visit *www.facthound.com*

Type in this code: 9781515726975

Check out projects, games and lots more at
www.capstonekids.com

INDEX

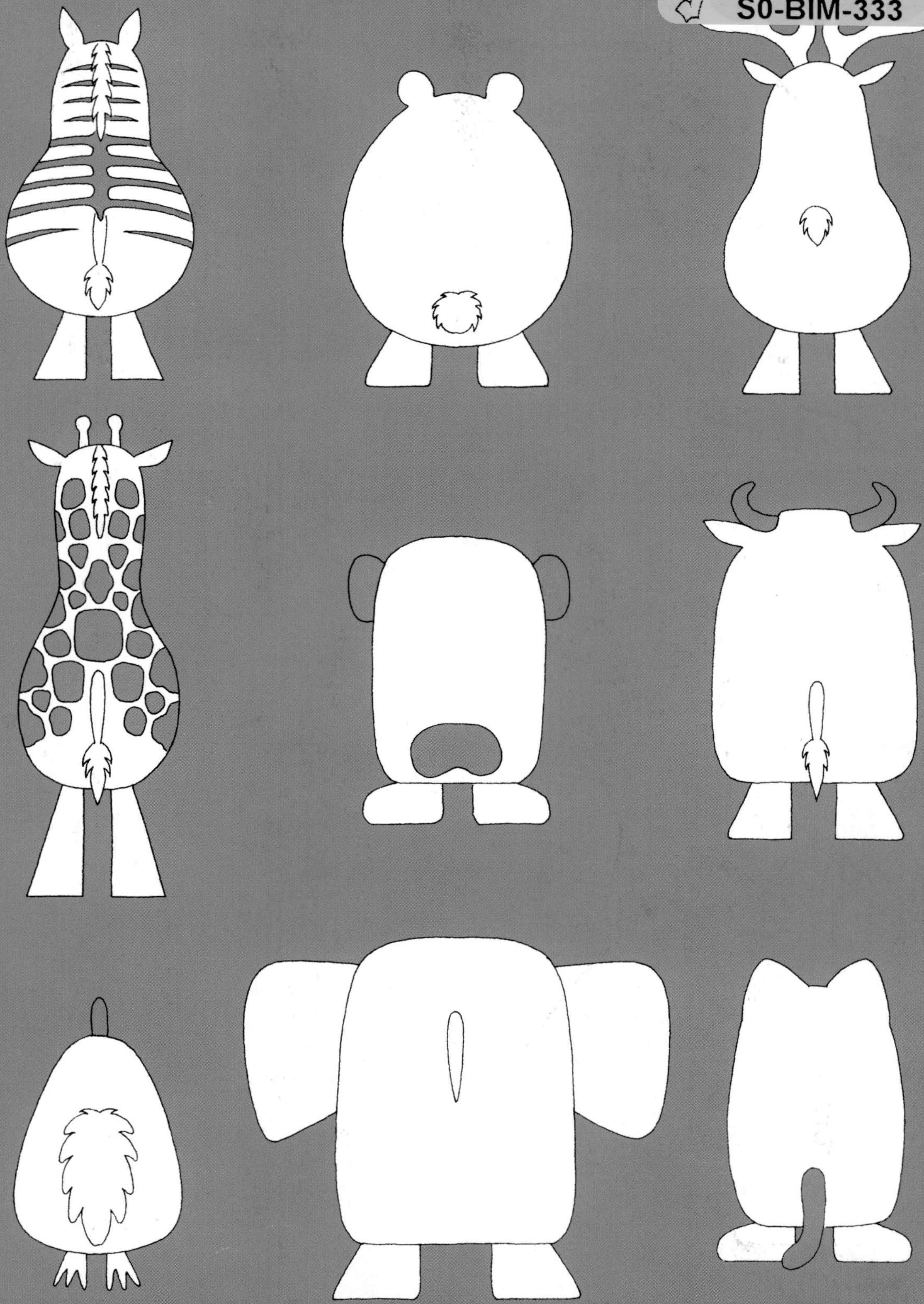

Who's Hiding?

Satoru Onishi

GECKO PRESS

Dog

Tiger

Hippo

Kangaroo

Lion

Rabbit

Rhino

Pig

Sheep

Zebra

Bear

Reindeer

Giraffe

Monkey

Bull

Hen

Elephant

Cat

3

Who's hiding?

Who's crying?

Who's hiding?

Who's angry?

Who's hiding?

Who has horns?

Who's hiding?

Who's backwards?

Who's hiding?

21

Who's sleeping?

Who's hiding?

Who's backwards?

Who's who?

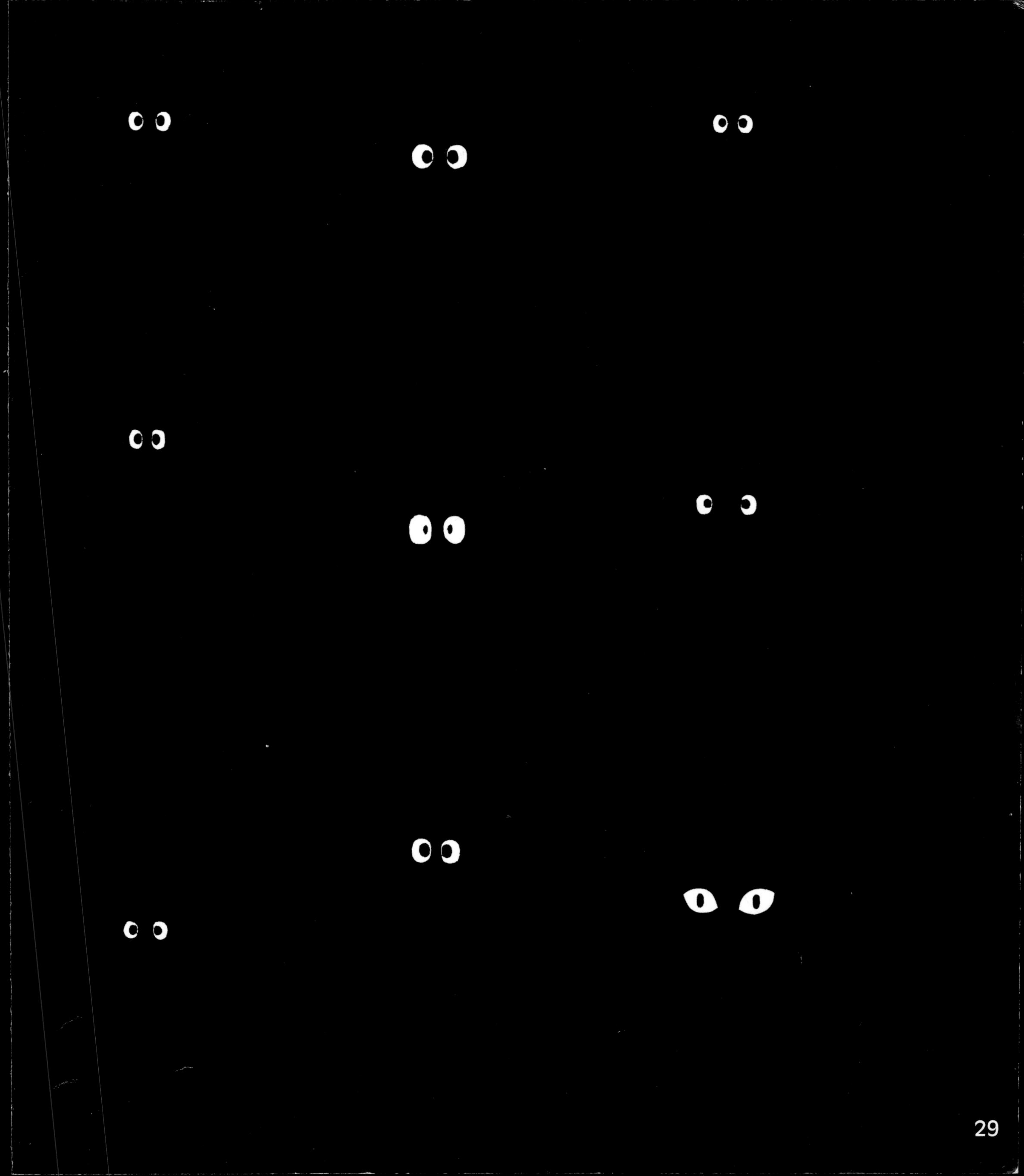

Dog

Tiger

Hippo

Kangaroo

Lion

Rabbit

Rhino

Pig

Sheep

Zebra

Bear

Reindeer

Giraffe

Monkey

Bull

Hen

Elephant

Cat

31

Answer Key

Pages 4–5	Reindeer is hiding.
Pages 6–7	Rabbit is crying.
Pages 8–9	Hippo is hiding.
Pages 10–11	Bear is angry.
Pages 12–13	Girrafe, Rhino, and Cat are hiding.
Pages 14–15	Reindeer, giraffe, Bull, Rhino and Sheep have horns
Pages 16–17	Dog, Lion, and Monkey are hiding.
Pages 18–19	Pig is backwards.
Pages 20–21	Bear, Rabbit, Pig, and Elephant are hiding.
Pages 22–23	Rhino is sleeping.
Pages 24–25	Tiger, Zebra, Kangaroo, Bull, Sheep, and Hen are hiding.
Pages 26–27	Tiger, Bear, Kangaroo, Lion, Monkey, Hen, and Cat are Backwards.
Pages 28–29	Dog, Tiger, Hippo, Zebra, Bear, Reindeer, Kangaroo, Lion, Rabbit, Giraffe, Monkey Bull, Rhino, Pig, Sheep, Hen, Elephant, Cat.

Page 1: Elephant

Kakureteiruno Dâre? © 1983 by Satoru Onishi
First published in Japan in 1983 by POPLAR Publishing Co., Ltd., Tokyo
English translation rights arranged with POPLAR Publishing Co., Ltd.
through Japan Foreign-Rights Centre

This edition first published in 2008 by Gecko Press
PO Box 9335, Wellington 6141, New Zealand
info@geckopress.com

Reprinted 2009, 2010, 2011 2012, 2013, 2014, 2015, 2017

English-language edition © Gecko Press Ltd 2008

Distributed in the United States and Canada by Lerner Publishing Group,
lernerbooks.com
Distributed in the United Kingdom by Bounce Sales and Marketing,
bouncemarketing.co.uk
Distributed in Australia by Scholastic Australia, scholastic.com.au
Distributed in New Zealand by Upstart Distribution, upstartpress.co.nz

Typesetting by Luke & Vida Kelly
Printed in China by Everbest Printing Co Ltd, an accredited ISO 14001
& FSC certified printer

ISBN hardback: 978-1-877467-12-7
ISBN paperback: 978-1-877467-13-4

For more curiously good books, visit geckopress.com